The Lamp of Love

Stories by Sathya Sai Baba

Edited by
David C. Jones
2010

Library and Archives Canada
Cataloguing in Publication

Sathya Sai Baba, 1926-
The lamp of love : stories by Sathya Sai Baba / selected, edited, and with an introduction by David C. Jones.

ISBN 978-1-55059-397-6

1. Love--Religious aspects--Hinduism--Quotations, maxims, etc. 2. Sathya Sai Baba, 1926- --Quotations. I. Jones, David C., 1943- II. Title.

BL1215.L68J66 2010
294.5'48677 C2010-903302-7

We recognize the support of the government of Canada through the Canada Books Program for our publishing program.

We also acknowedge the support of the Alberta Foundation of the Arts for our publishing program.

SAN 113-0234
ISBN 978-1-55059-397-6
Printed in Canada.
Cover design by James Dangerous.

Detselig Enterprises Ltd.

210 1220 Kensington Rd NW
Calgary, Alberta T2N 3P5
www.temerondetselig.com
temeron@telusplanet.net
p. 403-283-0900 *f.* 403-283-6947

Contents

Introduction

"SOMEONE PRAISED A YOUNG MAN PROFUSELY but added that he had only two tiny defects," said the Master. "So, he was chosen as the groom for the wedding, and after the ceremony was duly accomplished, it was discovered that that the two defects were: (1) he does not know anything; (2) he does not heed any one's advice."

"Most people suffer from this predicament," the Master added. "There is no independent thinking; there is no desire to learn."[1] No inclination to put into practice the good and the gracious.

The Master told another story of the state of his own country, India: "Father is happy with his second wife; children miserable with their step-mother." "The technological civilization of the West, the culture that places the standard of living in a more honourable place than the means by which that standard is attained, the culture that flies to the moon but is afraid to peep into the mind, has become the favourite wife; the children who are to be fed on mothers' milk of the eternal religion are miserable, for they have no training to secure it. Born to a rich heritage, the children are growing up destitute and helpless. Each one is the repository of Divine Might, of the Imperishable *Atma*. Contacting this Reality is the prime purpose of life. But, this is neglected; precious days are spent in inferior pursuits."[2]

The Master was Sathya Sai Baba, a man of miracles, born in 1926, and a teacher of wisdom, a weaver of stories, metaphorical and allegorical, about the nature and destiny of humanity. The *Atma* he spoke of was the eternal Spirit within, the Self, the breath of God that animated everyone: deathless, fadeless, ageless, infinite, indestructible, unbounded, unchanging, unlimited. Hard to describe a thing so vast and luminous, but it was really the Lamp of *Love*.

"Like the sun hidden by the clouds, embers covered by ash, the retina overlaid by cataract, the sheet of water veiled by moss, the consciousness of man is coated thick with likes and dislikes," said Baba; "how then can the splendour of *Atma* shine through?"[3] Other things block the *Atma* too: worries and fears, sloth and ignorance, ups and downs, frivolities and fevers, and conflicts and judgments, and more judgments, and most pointedly, the sense of *separateness*. "The Individual is the Universal pretending to be separate!" said Baba. And irony of ironies, even then he does not examine himself, the only thing he values. "You go millions of miles into space, but you don't go half-an-inch within, where lies your strength, the Supreme Power of the Self."[4] When people "have no time" for such inner plumbing and meditation, Baba calls it sheer "laziness." "How can any lower task claim the time that is legitimately the right of the one task for which man is born?"[5]

The one task is Self-discovery, a realization, magnificent and multiple, that perhaps begins with the understanding that the Self is more than the body. "The 'I' that lives within the body is like a lion in a cave," Baba teaches. "It is the monarch of the forest; but it limits itself to the few square feet of rocky floor. Let it come out, renouncing the petty possession. So long as you crib yourselves into the body-consciousness . . . you are the lion moping in the musty cave! Roar, I am *Brahman* (the Eternal, Changeless, divine Reality), I am all this and more, I am all this is, was, and will be—and littleness, time, space, ego, all will flee from our heart! You will be Love, Love, Love—and nought else."[6]

And Love is ever expanding, deepening its embrace, enlarging its kinship, ensuring the gentle mastery over oneself. "The real victory on which one can be congratulated," intones Baba, "is the victory over the six demons that have encamped in the mind of man, lust, anger, greed, attachment, pride and malice. When you do good deeds, keep good company, immerse your minds in good thoughts, these demons cannot survive in you."[7]

"Darkness will not flee if you throw stones at it; nor will it disappear if you lay about it with a sword, or shoot it with a gun," this Master teaches. "It will be destroyed only when a Lamp is lit."[8]

And the Lamp goes by different names, according to one's preference. Says Baba, "Some have faith only in Love, some believe only in Truth, some swear that they care only for Goodness—but all these do not know that they are referring to God alone by these names. They too are pilgrims to the same Sacred Shrine."[9]

The shrine is Wisdom, and Wisdom is but "compassion at its highest."[10]

David C. Jones

Endnotes

1 Sathya Sai Baba, *Sathya Sai Speaks*, vol. 15 (Prashaanti Nilayam, India: Sri Sathya Sai Books & Publications Trust, nd), 332, discourse, Dec. 30, 1982.

2 Ibid., vol. 7, 34, discourse, Mar. 3, 1967.

3 Ibid., vol. 20, 27, discourse, Feb. 26, 1987.

4 Ibid., vol. 14, 303, discourse, Sept. 21, 1980.

5 Ibid., vol. 7, 23, discourse, Jan. 22, 1967.

6 Ibid., vol. 7b, 75-76, discourse, Oct. 29, 1970.

7 Ibid., vol. 7, 127, discourse, May 23, 1967.

8 Ibid., vol. 3, 11, discourse, Apr. 28, 1963.

9 Ibid., vol. 7, 178, discourse, Oct. 7, 1967.

10 Ibid., vol. 11, 78, discourse, Jan. 22, 1967.

The Purpose of Life

The inherent nature of fire is "to burn"; of water, "to wet"; of stone, "to be heavy." The nature of man consists in the yearning "to know." This attribute has come into man from the moment he put on this body and entered the stage, to play the present role. SSS 7b, 47

Ten of them crossed a river, wading to the other bank. In order to find out whether all had arrived safe, one fellow counted the rest and declared there were only nine. Each of the ten counted the rest, and everyone agreed there were only nine survivors. One of them had definitely been drowned. So, the ten started wailing aloud in their bereavement, and a passerby was drawn to the group in sympathy. He saw there were ten, all right. The mistake was—the man who counted left himself out; he ignored himself, in counting the rest.

This is the mistake every one of these encyclopaedic intellects commit; they count everyone except themselves; they know everything except the workings of their own minds, and the methods by which they can attain inner calm. So, you must know who you are and then, if necessary, try to know about other persons and objects. Now it is all topsy-turvy. SSS 11, 222-23

You have wandered far and wide, but neglected your home. You peep into the stars in space, but keep your inner sky unexplored. You peep into other's lives and pick faults, and talk ill of them; but you do not care to peep into your own thoughts, acts and emotions and judge whether they are good or bad. The faults you see in others are but projections of your own; the good that you see in others is but a reflection of your own goodness. SSS 7, 117

You wear coloured glasses and see everything through those glasses. Correct your vision; the world will get corrected. Reform yourselves; the world will get reformed. You create the world of your choice. You see many, because you seek the many, not the One. Try to subsume the many in the One; the physical bodies of yourselves and others, the family, the village, the community, the state, the nation, the world. Thus progressively march on towards more and more inclusive loyalties and reach the stage of Unity, in thought, word and deed. This is the *Saadhana* [spiritual practice] of Love, for Love is expansion, inclusion, mutualisation. The individual has to be Universalised, expanded . . . . SSS 15, 37

The world is a huge hospital, and humanity is bedridden. Some are writhing in the pain of envy, some are bloated with pride, some are losing sleep through hate, some have become blind through miserliness, some are struck down by selfishness; everyone has some illness or other. SSS 2, 70

The fault lies in the belief that things happen as a result of human effort and planning, human intelligence and care. No one can succeed in any venture without Divine Grace. It is God's plan that is being worked out through man, but man prides himself that he has worked for it.

This reminds me of a story. A poor, simple villager made his first rail journey. He purchased a ticket and entered a compartment; he found it occupied already by a few passengers who had kept their boxes, bundles and odd items of luggage on the racks or under the benches on which they sat. They were unconcerned with the extra effort that the engine would have to make to drag along those boxes and bundles. How cruel of them, the villager thought. The engine has to pull along their weights, and now they are imposing on the train, this additional burden too. He for one was not going to inflict this extra trouble on the poor thing; so he kept his box on his shoulder and his bundle on his head. He believed that he was carrying his box and bundle along, and not the engine. Most people behave in the same silly fashion, ignoring the fact that God is All; man is but an instrument in His hands, for the execution of His Plan. Faith in this fact is the key to peace and joy. SSS 12, 274-75

Embodiments of the Divine *Atma* [the Divine Spirit]! Having achieved the rare fortune of a human body, one should ever strive to manifest the excellence which is its credential and to gain, as a result of that manifestation, Divinity Itself. When that is gained, nothing else need be gained. When the vision of That is won, there is nothing more to be visualised. When that is loved, nothing else would appear as worthy of love. All else would be trash and dust. When that is known, all is as good as known. SSS 17, 26

The Trueness of You

You must also see yourself, and hear your inner voice, urging you to discover your own truth. I am prompting you to discover your Reality. That is My Mission.

You were born for your own sake, not for the sake of any one else. You have to cure yourself of the disease of ignorance, just as you have to cure yourself of the disease of hunger. No one else can save you from both . . . . "Save yourself by yourself."

SSS 4, 274

There was a Guru (spiritual preceptor) once, who gave back to his pupils the fruits offered by them, with the direction, "Take, each one, what he likes most." One pupil did not take any fruit but sat unconcerned, in a corner. The Guru asked him, "What do you like most?" He answered, "Myself." That is the proper attitude; if you like yourself most, make the most of your self, know your self clearly and truly, revere your self deeply, be your best, make fullest use of your talents and skills, and lead yourself into lasting peace and joy. SSS 8, 72

Really, the power that man holds in himself is unsurpassed; no other created being has it. For he is the living image of God, the precious casket enshrining the Divine Itself. If you are weak, grief-stricken, and ignorant, the fault is yours; do not blame others: you have not tapped the spring of God within you. This is the sin—the turning of the blind eye to this patent fact. SSS 11, 130

Do not condemn your majesty bewailing, "I am unfortunate, I am despicable, I am downhearted." No. You are elated, you are enthroned, you are exalted. You are all this; but you are not aware of this, on account of *maya* (illusion). *Maya* is like your shadow in the well; if you do not peep into the well, it is not there! It is there, only whenever you peep into it. SSS 11, 36

Unite—in the One. That is your mission, your destiny. Do not isolate yourself—"I for me," "He for him." If you hope to be happy while isolated, take it from me, it is a frail dream. Know that you are the *Atma*, just as everything else is. The *Atma* is self-luminous; you do not need a lighted lamp to discover a lighted lamp! You need no candle or lantern to see the moon. You can see the moon through its own rays. The *Atma* shines in all; you have only to open your eyes and know it. The scriptures declare, "All this is God," "God is in all." Mere repetition of these truths as slogans is of no benefit; experience the Truth, live in the light of the Truth. SSS 15, 197-98

You will have observed that when your train is stationary, another train moving along another line gives you the feeling that it is your train that moves. If you watch your coach, fix your attention on your train, you know the truth. Similarly, as long as your attention is turned on "the other," "the outer," your knowledge is based on illusion. Once you divert the attention to yourself, you can discover the truth, viz., though the world moves you are still. SSS 2, 34

The Heart of Education

Purpose

Education should imbue students with certain ideals. They should realise that there is only one caste, the Caste of Humanity. There is only one religion, the Religion of Love. There is only one language, the Language of the Heart. SSS 19, 20

A college which does not confer the knowledge of their *Atmic* Reality to the students, engaged in the pursuit of various objectives and material studies, is as barren as a sky without the Moon, or a heart without peace, a nation without law. SSS 12, 137

Education must reveal the path which enables man to tap the dormant spring of divinity within, without getting entangled with the mass of created objects. It has to lay stress on spiritual transformation as more fundamental than even moral uplift. The real sign of an educated person is his attitude of sameness towards all. He sees in society the manifestation of divinity. Education does not lead from nature to the all pervading *Atma*. It leads man to study nature, with the unifying *Atmic* outlook. When the powers of Nature are harnessed to narrow selfishness, they recoil on him as plagues. When they are revered as revelations of the *Atma*, they become beneficial. Education equips man with this insight. The process by which man foregoes his freedom and is bound in the net of desire can never be education. It has to aim at ensuring peace and stability in each country by continuous precept and practice of the basic unity. SSS 19, 205

In Bangalore, many have known Sir C.V. Raaman. He is known all over India, too. He was a great scientist. When he was the Director of the Indian Institute of Science he had to interview candidates for jobs. One young man did not give the correct answers to some of his questions, and so, Raaman told him not to have hopes of securing the job. He advised him to try his luck somewhere else and asked him to leave. The candidate left the room slowly with a broken heart. He descended the steps and stood alone in the foyer. After some time, when Raaman came down, he noticed that he was still hanging around! He rebuked him and told him once again that he should give up all hopes of being taken for the job. The young man replied, with folded hands: "Sir! I am only waiting for the office to open. I have been paid five rupees extra by them as fare and daily allowance through wrong calculation. I shall return that amount and leave." On hearing this, Raaman's heart melted; he patted the candidate on his back; accepted him and gave him a job. Character is the best qualification. SSS 15, 101-02

Criticism

They are anxious to know all about what is happening in America or England. They wish to study Geography or Astronomy, but few are keen to find out their own true nature and their real essence. This is due to a defective education. In the present educational system, there is no place for ethical, dharmic, spiritual studies with the result that the students do not make any attempt to understand the purpose of human life. One seeks to learn all about the physical world. One learns all about America but does not know the route to Benares. One learns all about geometry, but knows little about the dimensions of his own house. One does all kinds of physical exercises but does not know how to sit in *Padhmaana* (Lotus posture). One studies Botany, but does not know the uses of the *Thulasi* (basic) plant. SSS 14, 330

A man engaged a boat to take him across the flooded Godavari. When the journey over the river started, he began a lively conversation with the boatman. He asked him whether he had any schooling, and when the reply came that he had none, he said sadly, "Alas! A quarter of your life has gone to waste. It is as if you have drowned those years in the Godavari." He asked him whether he could tell him the time from his watch: the boatman confessed he did not have a watch nor cared to have one. The Pundit deplored [that] and said, "Half your life has gone into the Godavari." His next question was about newspapers; did the boatman read any, what was his favourite paper? The boatman replied that he did not read any nor did he care to know the news. He had enough to worry about already. The Pundit declared forthright that three-quarters of the boatman's life had been liquidated. Just then the sky darkened with storm clouds, and there was an imminent threat of rain. The boatman turned to the Pundit: it was his turn to put a question. He asked, "Can you swim?" and when the frightened passenger confessed that he could not, the boatman said, "In that case, your entire life is now going to merge in the Godavari!" This is the case of the educated in India today. They do not have the training that will help them in distress, or in dire need, to win back their mental poise. SSS 3, 67-68

Mere mastery of books does not entitle a man to be called "educated." Without mastery over the inner instruments of emotions, no man can be deemed to be educated. SSS 14, 267

The educational system is beset with many problems. It has failed to promote in the young such qualities as love, forbearance and fortitude. Instead, it serves to encourage the animal nature in students. There is no place in it for cultivating human values like Truth and Righteousness. It does not imbue the student with a sense of humility, which is the hallmark of right education. SSS 19, 10-11

Education is being confused with the acquisition of verbal scholarship. This is wrong. Education has to open the doors of the mind. Many describe science today as a powerful acquisition, but science holds before mankind a great opportunity, that is all. It cannot be as great a power as it is imagined to be. If it is devoid of character, it brings disaster. It can then cause evil and wickedness. Intelligence can be found to be very high among clever thieves. So, too, scientific knowledge can be misused for destructive purposes. To enter Heaven, man must transform himself into an innocent infant. This is the Truth. To enter the heaven of science, man has to mould himself into a humble, unselfish seeker. SSS 15, 98

Einstein explained to a friend why he spent sleepless nights, and Gandhi too once gave the same reason to a questioner: "The hardness which the heart gains through education"! The friend told Einstein, "But you are a product of the same educational system." Einstein retorted, "I am what I am, not because of it but in spite of it!" Education has become a means to gain self-importance and boost one's conceit. SSS 15, 185

Teachers

Each mission requires a prime mover: you may have the lamp, oil, and wick, but someone must light it; you may have the flowers and the thread, but some person talented . . . must string them into a garland or form them into a bouquet; you may have both gold and the desire for jewels, but a smith with the skill must shape it into the coveted ornament; you may have the training and the yearning, but some Guru must provide the answer to the questions that torment you; and illumine you. SSS 7, 124-25

Bala Gangadhar Tilak, the great patriot and freedom fighter, who was in the teaching profession, was asked as to what position he would like to occupy when the country became independent. He replied that he was not interested in becoming a Minister or holding any office in the administration. He would prefer to go back to his profession of teaching so that he could mould several students into ministers or rulers rather than be a ruler himself. Such is the nobility and dignity of the teaching profession. SSS 19, 16

The true Guru is like an ophthalmic surgeon. The latter removes the film in the patient's eye and restores his natural vision. The Guru also should remove the veil of ignorance and attachment that blurs the vision of the disciple and restore his natural spiritual vision. SSS 16, 87

[Jesus] was born at 3:15 a.m. (early morning) on December 28, 1980 years ago. It was Sunday. The Star that appeared that day appears only once in 800 years. Its appearance had nothing to do with the birth of Jesus. There is no rule that, when Divine Energy or Divine Incarnation descends on Earth, a star has to appear. That is the opinion of devotees only. But, Jesus was himself a "Star" of infinite value, spreading brilliance of infinite dimension. Why posit another less brilliant glow? SSS 14, 257

Discourse, December 25, 1979

The Cultivation of Virtue

Attentiveness to God

God is as far from you as you are far from yourself. SSS 19, 98

Once upon time, Socrates was asked by a pupil, "Master! God has allotted a hundred years for man. But, he seldom lives so long. Twenty-five of them are spent in childhood, boyhood and youth playing silly games, 25 more in family and social entanglements and another 25 in allotting and apportioning properties among children. If he survives 75, he is ridden by disease or grief at the loss of son or daughter. He has no free time to think of God. It would be good if God grants 25 years more for him to dwell wholly in Him." Socrates responded with another equally sad statement. "Son! God has given us this vast house called Earth. But, three-quarters of it is sea; the other quarter is mostly mountain, desert, lake and forest. I have no place to live," he wept. The pupil consoled him: "Why? When billions can live on earth you surely can secure a place." Socrates said, "When so many billion thoughts are framed in your mind, my son, you can certainly find room easily for thoughts on God." Only idlers complain of want of time for meditating on God. "Yearn, you will find a way; pray, you will receive Grace." SSS 15, 112

You should cultivate an attitude of inseparable attachment to the Lord, who is your very self. If He is a flower, you should feel yourself a bee that sucks its honey; if He is a tree, be a creeper that clings to it; if a cliff, then feel that you are a cascade running over it; if He is the sky, be a tiny star that twinkles in it; above all, be conscious of the truth that you and He are bound by Supreme Love. SSS 5, 26-27

I shall give you one prescription which will give you the Peace and Contentment which you seek; it is Namasmarana. Install on the tongue any one of the thousand names of the Lord current in any part of the world, among any community of devotees. Repeat the Name for some time at least every day as part of your duty to yourself, a discipline which will yield good results, a habit which you should cultivate as a compensation for the hard toil that you do by your body from sunrise to sunset. SSS 3, 127

Whatever troubles you may face, whatever ordeals you may encounter, you should not allow your faith in God to weaken to the slightest extent. You must learn a lesson from the *Chakora* bird. There may be terrible thunder and blinding lightning in the sky. But the *Chakora* bird will follow the cloud to catch the raindrops in the sky and will not go to any other source for water. Nothing less than the pure raindrops from the cloud will satisfy the *Chakora*. Likewise, you should yearn always for the bliss of nearness to God, whatever difficulties or joys you may experience in life. SSS 19, 62

Ask any one the question—How do you provide for yourself in your old age? The answer will be, "O my son is well placed; I get the interest on my deposits; I have a pension; I have lands from which I can draw what I need," etc. But, no one answers, "I rely on God!" Without faith in God, without Divine help, how can any of these give succour during the stormy voyage through life's declining years? Faith in God is the secure foundation on which hope has to be built. SSS 7a, 245

A merchant was once hauled before a magistrate for selling adulterated ghee [liquid butter] which smelt bad and was a danger to health. Judgment was pronounced that he should either himself consume the entire quantity of ghee as a punishment, receive 20 stripes or pay a fine of 100 *varaahas* (gold coins). He preferred the ghee and started drinking the stuff; but finding the smell was unbearable, he chose the stripes. He received about a dozen but he could not stand more. So, he finally told the magistrate that he might be let off with the fine. If only he had opted for it first, he could have avoided the foul drink and the excruciating pain. By his indecision, he had to taste the reek and the rod.

Similarly man does not opt for God in the beginning, when grief overtakes him. He has to opt for God, sooner or later; but he does not recognize the inevitability. Choose wisely. SSS 6. 119

Abou Ben Adhem found that the Angel had recorded his name in the list of those whom God loved, though his name was nowhere to be found in the register of those who loved God; for, he loved, not God, but men. That is enough to win Grace.
SSS 7a, 198

Many people hope to lead good lives by doing good deeds. But I do not believe this is possible. You can never become good, by means of good deeds. You have to be good, in order that your deeds and words can be good. First, endeavour to be a good person. Thereafter, it becomes possible for you to do good. Be good; do good. SSS 14, 310

Attentiveness to Nature

Learn a lesson from the tree. When it is heavy with fruits it does not raise its head aloft in pride; it bends low, stoops, as if it does not take any credit for its accomplishment and as if it helps you to pluck the fruit. Learn a lesson from the birds. They feed those who cannot fly far; the bird relieves the itch of the buffalo by scratching with its beak; they help and serve each other, with no thought of reward. SSS 8, 10

The sandalwood tree will lend its fragrance even to the axe which cuts it down. That is the nature of the good and the great.
SSS 7, 222

Attentiveness to Your Own Experience

Do not give ear to what others say. Believe your experience. What gives you peace and joy . . . believe in that. That is the real basis for faith. Why should you go about asking all and sundry whether something is either salt or sugar? Is it not foolish to wander about consulting people about this? Put a little on your own tongue; that will settle the matter. What you are now doing is to reject as salt what your own experience has proved to be sugar, simply because someone who has not tasted it like you proclaims it to be salt or because someone who is down with a fever finds the thing bitter. SSS 6, 122

Attentiveness to the Body

The body has to be kept trim until this [self-realization] is achieved; its purpose too is just this. Keep it light and bright. It is a boat which can take you across the sea of illusion, of false multiplicity. Don't add to its weight by attachment to things and others; then, it is in danger of sinking during the voyage. SSS 5, 256

Company of the Good

There were two parrots on a tree, twins to be more precise. A hunter trapped them and sold them, one to a low, cruel butcher and the other to a sage who was running an ashram to teach the Vedas. After a few years, he was surprised to find that one bird swore very foully, while the other recited the leelas of the Lord in a sweet musical tone which captivated the listeners. Such is the effect of the environment: so, seek and secure *Satsang* (holy company). SSS 1, 93

Seeking good company and spending all available time in that comradeship called *Satsang*, will help the aspirant a great deal. You are shaped by the company you keep; a piece of iron turns into rust if it seeks the company of the soil. It glows, it softens and takes on useful shapes if it enjoys the company of fire. Dust can fly if it chooses the wind as its friend; it has to end as slime in a pit if it prefers water. It has neither wing nor foot, yet it can either fly or walk, rise or fall, according to the friend it selects. SSS 13, 141

Here is an episode from the *Mahabharata*. Once, when his wife, Subhadra, was enceinte, Arjuna, not knowing that the child she was bearing was the future hero Abhimanyu, began telling her all about warfare and the Padmavyuha, an intricate type of military formation, Krishna came in at that time and pointed out to Arjuna that the child Subhadra was carrying was being influenced by what he was telling her. It is an ancient practice in Bharat [India] to relate to pregnant women stories about heroes and saints so that the child in the womb may be influenced by the vibrations produced by such sublime stories and the thoughts produced in the mother. The ancient *Rishis* knew this truth. No wonder that the children born under such conditions had noble nature and heroic virtues. SSS 18, 150

Detachment

Zoroaster, one day, asked the Prince of Iran, "Go, light this lamp, from yonder flame." The lamp could not be lit; for the wick was soaked in water. Then Zoroaster said, "Your mind is so soaked in desire that it cannot receive the wisdom it needs; dry it in the sun of detachment." When teachers and the taught are immersed in worldly desire, how can light be transmitted or kept alive? SSS 7, 145

Determination

When a man falls into a well, of what use is it if he controls his voice and his emotions and whispers quietly, "I have fallen into this well, I have fallen into this well. I am in great danger. Please save me"? No one will be able to hear or save him. He must shout full-throated, with all the anguish he is experiencing and with the extreme desire to be saved, "I HAVE FALLEN INTO THE WELL! SAVE ME, SOME ONE!" Then can he hope to get succour.

Similarly, when you are caught in the coils of this world, when you have fallen into this deep well of worldly misery, shout with all your might, with all your heart, that you may be saved by God. There is no use muttering faintly and half-heartedly, "Save me, save me; I am floundering in this *samsaara* (worldly life)." When the prayer comes shrieking through the heart, help is assured. SSS 13, 134-35

Devotion

Uddhava was an adept in the path of *Jnana Yoga* (Knowledge and Wisdom). He wanted to teach the *gopikas* (the cowherdesses) the path of Wisdom. So, he approached Krishna. Krishna told Uddhava: "The *gopikas* are totally devoted to me. Their devotion is fundamental to their life and reaches My heart! Their purity and devotion are like a light that shines! You cannot understand the hearts of such devotees! I am completely enshrined in their hearts." Uddhava doubted whether ignorant, illiterate *gopikas* could understand the Divine. To dispel the doubts of Uddhava, Krishna sent him to Repalle. Uddhavea summoned the *gopikas* and told them: "I will teach you the path of Jnana to realize the Divine." The *gopikas* came to Uddhava and told him: "We are not interested in learning any *sastras!* Teach us one simple means by which we can realise Krishna! We are not aware of any yoga or *bhoga* or mantra. Krishna is everything for us, our yoga or *bhoga*. Please, therefore, tell us the means by which we can obtain Krishna! We do not want to waste our time on yoga."

Uddhava asked the *gopikas*: "How can you become one with Krishna?" One *gopika* answered: "If Krishna were a flower, I would be a bee whirling round Him. If He were a tree, I would be a creeper twining round him. If He were a mountain, I would be a river cascading from its top! If Krishna were the boundless sky, I would be a little star, twinkling in the firmament. If He were the deep ocean, I would be a small stream, joining the ocean. This is the way I would be one with Krishna and merge with Him." Another *gopi* said: "If Krishna were a flower, I would be a bee which goes on sucking every drop of honey in the flower tasting the nectar that is there! This is our approach to God." So, spiritual *sadhana* [practice] means to regard a mountain or a tree, or a flower, or the ocean, as a means of God-realization. SSS 18, 200-01

Dharma

The agonizing years of torment, hope, and disillusion were over; the moment of decision had come, though it was sought now by the sharp edge of the sword and not the soft words of Lord Krishna. The armies gathered by the Kauravas from their kingdom and from their allies were standing face to face with the forces of their Pandava cousins.

Cavalry, chariotry, elephantry and infantry, eager to start the destruction of the enemy, the chief actors all dressed and equipped for the fray! Conches were blown; trumpets rent the sky with their blare. The air was tense with hope, fear, anxiety and anger. Blood in a million bodies became redder and warmer; hearts pounded quicker; arms grasped weapons in deadly grip.

Dharmaraja, the eldest of the Pandava brothers, suddenly removed his footwear; he laid aside his armour; he slid from his chariot; he walked towards the opposing cohorts, towards Bheeshma, the Generalissimo of the enemy forces. Duryodhana, the eldest of the Kaurava brothers, the cousin most responsible for the war, the unyielding opponent of the Pandavas, saw Dharmaraja cross over to the aged Bheeshma. He was overjoyed; he guessed that Dharmaraja had decided on surrender, for he was by nature against bloodshed and battles.

The four brothers of Dharmaraja were astounded. Bheema, the redoubtable hero of a hundred contests with the Kauravas, the person most eager for the battle to begin, felt foiled of victory. He recalled the many occasions when Dharmaraja had stood in the way of revengeful action against the Kauravas. He feared that he would apologise and withdraw like a craven from the bloody gamble of war. Arjuna, the formidable bowman, witnessed his brother's defection with horror and anger. Nakula and Sahadheva, the twins, were struck dumb at their own helplessness.

Lord Krishna studied the situation from the seat of the charioteer on the chariot of Arjuna, which was in the front line of the Pandava army. He signed to the four of them to follow their eldest brother and do likewise. He said, "All these years you have revered him, and trod on his footsteps. So go now. Do not hesitate; do not doubt." Dharmaraja was the very embodiment of Dharma (right action); he knew the right and he practised it whatever the consequences. He knew that Dharma will guard those who follow Dharma. He never did a hypocritical or a non-Vedhic act; he never took a wrong step. He went straight to Bheeshma and fell at his feet. Standing before him with folded hands and bowed heard, he prayed. "Grandfather! We had no chance to experience the love of the father; he passed away too soon. You brought us up from infancy with love and care, and made us what we are today. We have no right to fight against you; but fate has conspired to bring us now into battle with you. Please have mercy on us; permit us to raise our arms against you."

Bheeshma was naturally charmed and overjoyed at the humility and righteousness of Dharmaraja; his eyes were filled with tears at the strange turn that destiny had taken; he blessed him and said, "Dharmaraja! You have stuck to Dharma, in spite of the temptations this situation has placed before you. What a noble example you have set before the world! This Dharma that you follow will itself give you victory."

Next, Dharmaraja and the brothers moved towards General Drona, the Brahmin Preceptor, who had taught archery to both the Kauravas and their cousins, the Pandavas. Dharmaraja fell at his feet too and prayed. "Highly revered Preceptor! We five are your pupils; how can we rightfully take up arms against our Preceptor? The times have indeed gone awry. Pardon us, for this wrong. Permit us to engage with you in battle." Drona, the *Aacharya*, [spiritual teacher] was visibly moved by this appeal. "Ah! How great and good, this Dharmaraja is! Even at this moment when the hounds of war are to be let loose to spread death and fury, he is sticking to the dictates of Dharma!" Drona was thrilled at the thought. He clasped Dharmaraja in his arms and said, "Son! You are dearer to me than Aswathaama [his own son] for, I am drawn to him only by duty, whereas I am drawn to you by love. You are all my sons, for, I love you as such. Your right will certainly earn victory over our might."

It is this adherence to Dharma that ensured their victory. Or else, was there any one on earth at that time who could force the redoubtable Bheeshma to lay down his arms? Could any one excel Drona in archery? The Kauravas, whom Bheeshma and Drona sought to support were defeated because they trod the path of adharma (vice), while the Pandavas never deviated from the path of Dharma. Dharma gave them the skill, strength, courage and tenacity to defeat these great masters of military strategy.

The Kauravas went counter to their parents and their God. Their mother, Gaandhaari, counseled her children, in a thousand ways, not to continue their vendetta against their cousins, the Pandavas. But they did not heed her. Their father Dhritarashtra pleaded with them to desist from the path of hate; but to no avail. They turned a deaf ear to the advice offered by their Preceptor, Drona, to make peace with the Pandava cousins and give them their legitimate share of the realm. When the Lord, Sri Krishna Himself, went to them as a messenger of peace, as an Ambassador with the Mission of Peace, they refused to listen to His Divine words; they attempted even to overpower Him and put Him into bonds!

If you follow the same line of willful blindness, you will have to meet the same fate—total destruction. SSS 12, 214-17

The temptation to ignore Dharma grows from egoism and the acceptance of false values. The wish to satisfy the lower desire is the root of adharma. This wish takes hold of you slyly, like a thief in the night; or like a comrade come to save you; or like a servant come to attend on you; or, like a counselor come to warn you. Oh, the wickedness has a thousand tricks to capture your heart. You must be ever alert against the temptation. The wish makes a chink in your consciousness, enters and establishes itself and then multiplies its brood and eats into the personality you have built up with laborious care. The fort is no longer under your control. You have been reduced into a puppet manipulated by these inner enemies. Whenever you try to rebuild yourselves, they undermine the structure, and you have to do it all over again. This is the extent of the harm they do. SSS 3, 232-33

When you attempt to deceive another, remember there will emerge someone who can deceive even you. There was a thief once who was skilled in all the stratagems and tricks of that profession. There was not a single one that he had not mastered. One day, after collecting a large number of costly articles and bundling them up, he was moving along a lonely road with the booty on his shoulder. He saw a child standing on the bank of a wayside tank, weeping aloud, in great distress. The thief went near and asked, "Why are you weeping? What has happened to you?" The child said, (and here, you have to remember that it does not matter how old or how young a person is, it is the intelligence that matters) "I came here for a bath, my golden necklace fell into the waters, right there, where I tried to have a dip. The place is too deep for me."

The thief thought that he could get away with this necklace too, for it was a little child that stood between him and the jewel. So, placing his bundle on the bank, he went down into the waters to retrieve the necklace. Meanwhile, the child lifted the thief's bundle and running a short distance, disappeared into the jungle. The thief came up disappointed, for the necklace was but a fiction, only to find that he had been robbed! Whoever deceives another will have some one cleverer, to outwit him. SSS 7b, 109-10

You believe that God guards the good from harm and inflicts on the bad; that is not correct. The goodness of the good guards them; the badness of the bad injures them. God is the Witness.
SSS 7, 130

Discipline

When you build a house, you install a door in front. What is the purpose of the door? To admit all whom you welcome and to keep out all whom you do not want. It has a double purpose; you do not keep the doors wide open, for all and sundry to come in as and when they like. So too, select the impulses, the motives, the incentives that enter your mind; keep out the demeaning, the debasing, the deleterious. SSS 3, 144

Life is a jungle, where there is a great deal of dry wood which harbours worms and insects. No one cleans the floor of the forest, or cuts away the undergrowth of bush and bramble. To wade through the thorns and the leech-ridden floor of the jungle, one has to wear boots. So too, one has to wear the boots of sense-regulation if one has to pass through the jungle of life without harming oneself. This is the lesson I want you to carry home with you today, for pondering over and for practice.
SSS 7, 111

Equanimity

The most precious possession is mental equanimity; and it is the one thing you cannot give, even if you have it. Each has to acquire it the hard way. SSS 16, 163s

Buddha . . . brought home to them another lesson. He asked one of them: "Child! A beggar comes to your house asking for alms: 'Blessed mother, give me food!' You bring some food. If the beggar says, 'This is not the alms I asked for, and I will not accept it,' what will you do?" The man replied: "I will keep back the offering." Buddha said: "In the same manner, you attempted to offer me the *bhiksha* (alms) of your abuse. I did not accept it. To whom does it belong? It remains with you. So, you have only abused yourself, not me," said Buddha.

If a registered letter is addressed to some one who declines to receive it, the postal department will deliver it back to the sender. Similarly, if you criticise someone or hate somebody, if the other person remains unaffected and unperturbed, your criticism and hatred come back to you. SSS 17, 131

Fortune is as much a challenge to one's equanimity as misfortune. SSS 18, 108

Faith

One evening Krishna took Arjuna far out of Dwaraka City and while they were alone together, He pointed at a bird flying over their head and asked him, "Arjuna, isn't that a dove?" Arjuna agreed; he said it was a dove. Suddenly, Krishna turned towards him and said, "No, it is a crow." Arjuna concurred and said, "I am sorry, it certainly is a crow." Immediately, Krishna asked him, "A crow, no, it must be a kite. Is it not so?" and Arjuna promptly agreed. "Yes. It is a kite." At this, Krishna smiled and asked Arjuna, "Are you in your senses? What exactly do you see? Why you say, of the same bird, it is a dove, it must be a crow and it is a kite?" Arjuna said, "Who am I to dispute your statement? You can make it a crow even if it is not one, or, change it into a kite. I have found that the safest thing is to agree with you, in full faith. I know of no other course." It was only after this test for unflinching faith that Krishna assured himself of the credentials of Arjuna to receive the [Bhagavad] Geetha advice.
SSS 7, 211-12

Faith is power. Without faith, living is impossible. We have faith in tomorrow following today. That is what makes us take up activities and projects that extend beyond this day. People with no faith cannot plan; they court misery by their want of faith. A rich man in South Africa once heard a divine voice which promised him a gold mine, if only he would dig at a certain place. He dug at that place to a depth of 200 feet and failed to discover any vein of gold. His faith waned. He doubted the authenticity of the voice. He talked to others how the voice had played false. When another rich man heard his story, he developed great faith in what he believed to be God's command. He dug in the same areas and laid bare a rich gold mine barely three feet below the surface of the earth. That became the richest and the most famous of the gold mines of South Africa.

During the Second World War, a steamer carrying Indian sepoys was bombed by the Japanese, and it was sunk. Many lost their lives. Only five men managed to row their life-boat and hoped to have a chance to survive, in spite of the surging ocean. They were tossed about for many hours. One of them became desperate. "The sea will swallow me. I will be food for sharks," he cried, and, in panic, he fell into the sea. Another sepoy wept for his family. "I am afraid they will suffer much. I am dying without arranging for their future," he said. He too lost his faith in his survival and breathed his last. The third man said, "Alas! I have with me the policy documents of insurance. What a pity I did not give them to my wife. How can she get the amount, now that I am dying?" And he also died.

The other two men reinforced each other's faith in God. They said, "We shall prove by sticking to life, however desperate the situation. God has created us for some good purpose. We shall not yield to fear. We shall not give up faith in God's compassion and power." They had to give up the leaky boat and swim towards the shore. Within five minutes, a helicopter sent from a coastal ship, which had received signals for help from the sinking steamer, sighted them and hauled them up to safety. While safe on land, they said, "It is only five minutes between victory and defeat." Those who dug for the gold mine could well say, "It is only three feet of soil between victory and defeat." Faith won the victory; want of it brought about defeat and death. SSS 15, 64-65

Life is impossible without breath. Life is also impossible without faith. All of you who have come to this gathering came here in the faith that you can return home. If that faith was absent, you would not have come at all. Some declare, "Experience first, faith next." This is similar to the declaration, "Swim first, water next." Have faith enough to practise the advice; learn to revere the directives. Then you attain the experience. How can the stomach be full without eating the meal? So, take up the effort. Plunge into action. Do not hesitate or doubt. Action, that is the Divine Task. That is the reason why the very first section of the *Vedhas* is the *Karma Kaanda*, the "Stage of Action." SSS 15, 143

Faith is the very foundation for any forward step. If the step has to await the dawn of faith through experience, one cannot progress at all. SSS 17, 49

False Attachment

This is the story of a man who was bathing in the Godhavari when it was in spate. As he was bathing he saw a stick with a golden handle floating towards him. He caught hold of it and left it on the bank to complete his bath. Meanwhile, the bank caved in and the stick was carried away by the river. After his bath, the man found the stick missing and wailed over his loss. There was no reason for his elation in getting the stick or his grief over the loss. It did not belong to him. It was a chance acquisition, and it left him in the manner it had come. Why claim any right to it? The temporary attachment to the stick was a bondage that subsequently caused grief. If there had been no attachment, there would have been no sorrow. SSS 20, 23

Only beggars are prompted by the urge to gather riches.
SSS 14, 240

The mind urges the senses to seek and secure softness, sweetness, fragrance, melody and beauty, not in God whose heart is soft as butter, whose story is sweet as nectar, whose renown is fragrant as the jasmine, whose praise is melodious to the ear, whose Form is the embodiment of perfect beauty, but, in the shoddy contraptions of material things. So, the mind has to die, so that it may be recast as an instrument for liberation, through fulfillment. SSS 5, 287

The deer is trapped, the elephant is drawn into the *kheddah* (the trap), and the serpent is charmed—all by taking advantage of their slavery to the senses. SSS 5, 302

False Devotion

I am reminded of an old widow who shed tears for hours on end listening to a *Pandith* who was expounding the Geetha. At the end of the series of discourses, when the *Pandith* had finished the Valedictory *Puuja* [worship], he called the old widow near the altar and publicly acclaimed her as a sincere seeker of the Godly Path, for she was the most punctual, the most earnest and the most devoted among the hundreds of listeners, as was evidenced by the tears she shed whenever the words of the Lord were referred to. The old lady was surprised at all this. She said she had understood not a word; she did not know what the Geetha was or said; she shed tears because the black string with which the palm leaf text of the Geetha in the hands of the *Pandith* was tied reminded her of the cord round the waist of her departed husband! SSS 6, 53-54

Spiritual effort should not become mechanical repetition of set formulae or execution of dry formalities. A sage who lived long ago had a cat in his hermitage; whenever he performed a *homa* (offering oblations to gods into the consecrated fire), the cat frisked around the Fire and gave a lot of trouble to him. So he used to catch it in advance and keep it under an inverted basket for the duration of the *homa*. His son who watched this operation for years thought that this cat-catching and cat-imprisonment were vital parts of the ritual itself. So he took great trouble to seek out a cat before every *homa* and felt happy when he got one which he could keep under an inverted basket in the same room. This is an example of meaningless mechanicalisation.
SSS 7, 7

False Focus

A number of people have handed over questions to Me regarding the nature of the mind. So, though I have often explained this in my discourses, I shall speak about it again. You are all now in Prashaanthi Nilayam, gathered in this hall; but, if your mind is wandering in Madras or Calcutta, you will not be seeing the man sitting in the line before yours, or hear Me speak, though I am speaking so loud! Though your eyes and ears are present here, effective and sound, if your mind is not controlling them and directing them, the senses are powerless . . . . The operations of hearing, smelling, seeing, tasting and getting the feel of touch, cannot be done effectively and meaningfully if the mind is engaged otherwise! SSS 7b, 100

The fly rests one moment on the sacred food-offerings on the altar of God and the next moment on filth. The mind seeks refuge in holy thoughts and things; the next moment, it revels in some fearsome, foul ideas. The mind is like the elephant. The mahout gives it a nice bath, he scrubs it clean and chains it to a shady tree. But, it gathers dust with its trunk and scatters it all over itself! Man too, urged by the senses, pours into his own mind dust and dirt. SSS 15, 251

The mind has to be completely emptied of all bad thoughts to achieve real peace. Every bad thought must be rooted out the moment it arises in the mind. The war against bad thoughts is like the war against enemy hordes who attempt to get behind a fort through a subterranean tunnel. As each one of the enemy emerges from the tunnel, he should be struck down. Each one of the sense organs—the eye, the tongue or the ear—when it is influenced by a bad thought, is led astray and behaves improperly. When they are influenced by good thoughts and impulses, they act in a manner which produces joy and contentment. When the eye sees someone who is regarded as an enemy, there is an upsurge of ill-will in the mind. On the other hand, when one sees a dear friend the reaction is one of love and affection. SSS 19, 120

When one wish is fulfilled, ten rise in its place. For, there is no dearth of want; the same person has come to Me seeking success at the examination, then a job, then a father-in-law, then a child, then a raise in the salary, a transfer to a cheaper place, a seat in the Medical College for the son—a never-ending series of wants, until at last, he comes seeking My Grace for an end to worldly pursuits and for initiation into the path of spiritual liberation! *Chintha* (anxiety) is what such people dwell on. *Chintha* means, in Telugu, the tamarind tree. They dwell on the tamarind tree, the *Chintha* tree; but, My tree is the "*Santhosha* tree, the Tree of Joy." SSS 5, 63

False Love

When Raavana fell dead, his queen Mandodhari lamented over his body, "You conquered every enemy of yours, except your own lust! You were pious, you were learned, you subdued even the most powerful foes—but, you allowed yourself to be enslaved by desire. That brought about your downfall."
SSS 7, 182-83

False Progress

I am reminded of what Hussain, the son of Rabbia Malik of Persia used to do. He rose early and went to the mosque for prayers with great diligence and devotion. When he came back, he found the servants of the house still sleeping on their mats, and he grew wild at them; he swore and cursed them for neglect of religious duties. Then his father chastised him. He said, "Son, why do you get angry with those poor souls who are too tired to wake up early. Do not wipe off the good results of your adherence to the rule of God by falling foul of these innocent slaves. I wish you would much rather rise late and abstain from the mosque, for now you have grown proud that you are more religious than these others and you dare blame them for faults for which they are not themselves responsible." SSS 1, 54-55

Do not envy the countries that are attempting to reach the Moon and Mars and to explore the reaches of outer space. Of what avail is it to master those regions while remaining slaves to every gust of malice or fear? Of what avail is it to travel at ten thousand miles per hour with a mind weighed down by dark impulses of the savage past? SSS 2, 132

False Renunciation

[King Sikhadhwaja] got a feeling of extreme renunciation and left for the forest for ascetic practices. His queen Choodala had the spirit of detachment in greater measure, but she did not make a show of it as her husband did.

The queen put on male attire, wore ochre, spelt a rosary and sought him in the jungle. Discovering him at last, she asked him who he was. The king replied that he was the ruler of the realm, that he had given up his riches, his treasure, his army, his court, etc. "For the sake of what did you give up these?" asked Choodala. "For the sake of peace," replied the king. But, he had to confess that he had not attained it. Then, Choodala taught him that the giving up of "things" will bear no fruit, that the desire for things, the pride of possessing things, of having once possessed them, has to be given up, that one must be detached from the objective world so that he might turn his eyes inward and conquer the foe of the inner realm and become a master of himself. When the king attempted to fall at the feet of the new Guru that had come to him, Choodala revealed her identity. She was a *sati* (virtuous wife) who was the Guru of her *pati* (husband); there were many such women in ancient times . . . SSS 4, 142-43

False Sacrifice

In *Vedhic yajnas* [rituals] patronized by those who consider the letter to be sacrosanct, a lamb is sacrificed, and its diaphragm offered as an oblation . . . The *Vedhic* myth or concept is clothed in symbols. A symbol, like the word "diaphragm" is capable of a wide range of interpretations, both allegoric and metaphoric.

The young of the sheep is as tender as the human baby. It is innocence personified, full of charming playfulness. Sheep are docile and harmless, incapable of injuring others. The lamb is as holy as the purest of angels. The diaphragm which separates the thoracic from the abdominal cavities is only a symbol of the layer of *jnaana* [wisdom] which separates the worldly from the spiritual. It represents the casket in which the pure *saathwik* [soft-natured] heart is enshrined. God will accept such an offering, and not inferior oblations. What is therefore meant by the text is that one has to maintain the heart as the source and repository of pure love and offer it to God. There was no intention to slaughter the dear little lamb. Be a lamb; offer the innocent heart encased in Love—that is the message. What can mortal man gain by killing another mortal being? SSS 15, 296-97

Another devotee . . . said to me: "Rather than lead the kind of life I am leading, I would prefer to commit *Atma-hatya* (end myself)." He said he was being oppressed by many doubts. I told him: "What is it that suffers from doubts? It is the mind. You want to commit *Atma-hatya,* put an end to your life, for the faults of the mind. This means you are punishing the body for the offences of the mind. You will be committing a grievous wrong if you punish the innocent body for the crimes of the errant mind." The devotee felt sorry and prayed to be forgiven. SSS 20, 189

False Surrender

There are some who declare glibly, “O, I have surrendered my body, mind, intellect, my everything to God.” These people have no control over their minds and the emotions and passions they are filled with. They have no mastery over their reason. They are not even able to regulate their bodies. So, it is indeed ridiculous for them to claim that they have offered them to God. How can they give to God what is not theirs? What right have they? How can anyone accept the gift of something which does not belong to the giver? SSS 12, 15

False Wisdom

Believe—strive—succeed; that is the message of the sacred texts. But the texts are not put to these uses by those who handle them. They are read for disputative ends, for pedantic display of intricate scholarship; or as some people do, they are worshipped as holy relics of the past. They are seldom adopted as guides for daily life, as life-belts during the perilous sea voyage called life. The Raamayana, the Mahaabhaaratha, the Bhaagavatha are mastered, but not allowed to become master. You go through them without allowing them to go through you! The volumes are bound in silk, and incense sticks are burnt before them, while man prostrates before them in reverence. But no attention is paid to what the pages proclaim. The frills and fringes attract the mind, more than the kernel provided by the text. SSS 6, 53

Happiness

Another illusion is happiness consists in accumulating money or knowledge or comforts or reputation. Trying to be happy through such accumulation is like getting into the Madras Bus and hoping to reach Bangalore. What is happiness? It is the state of mind, which is unaffected by fortune, good or bad. By systematic education, the mind can attain that state. If activity is done as worship, then, the mind will be steady and free from anxiety. SSS 7a, 219-20

Health and Healing

Raamakrishna Paramahamsa told an addict that he must not consume more than a given quantity of opium; he gave him a piece of chalk, to weigh every day the quantity of opium he [could] eat—no more, no less! But he imposed a condition, whose usefulness in helping him to conquer the bad habit the addict did not realize then. It was that every time he used the weight he had to write on a slate, the *Pranava (Om),* before putting it on the scale of the balance. The fellow obeyed; the chalk was reduced in weight with every *Om*, until it was eliminated in full; the opium habit too was reduced out of existence! The *Om* also helped to transfer his attachment from the opium-inducing tranquility to the everlasting Bliss of God-intoxication.

SSS 7, 220-21

There are some who are puzzled at the sight of a hospital here. They imply that everything here should be done through some miracle or some strange inexplicable manner! It also implies that no one who has come here should fall ill or die. I have no desire that you should live; or fear that you may die. It is you that decide your condition. All have to die, sooner or later. No one will be anxious to have the same dress on for years and years. Death is but the casting off of old clothes. When even *Avathaars* leave the body after the Task is fulfilled, how can man be saved from inevitable dissolution? The hospital is for those who believe in the doctor and in drugs. It is faith that matters, that cures. It also serves to accommodate those who are too ill to move about, but, yet come over to this place for cure. SSS 9, 112-13

The manner and mien of the physician are more effective in drawing out the latent sources of strength in the patient, than the most powerful drug. A prayerful atmosphere of humility and veneration will go a long way to help the cure. We may say that the behaviour, the voice, the mien of the doctor count for fifty per cent of the cure, the drugs and their efficacy manage the other half. SSS 14, 298

A Sanyasi [monk] once met the Cholera Goddess on the road, returning from a village where she had thinned the population. He asked her how many she had taken into her lap; she replied, "Only ten." But, really speaking, the casualties were a hundred. She explained, "I killed only ten; the rest died out of fear!"
SSS 3, 177

Disease has its hold on every family, in every home . . . The reason is, the atmosphere in the modern home is filled with artificiality, anxiety, envy, discontent, empty boasting, vain pomp, extravagance, falsehood and hypocrisy. How can anyone growing up in this corrosive atmosphere be free from illness?
SSS 7, 168

Illness, both physical and mental, is a reaction on the body caused by poisons in the mind. An uncontaminated mind alone can ensure continuous health. Vice breeds disease. Bad thoughts and habits, bad company and bad food are fertile grounds where disease thrives. *Aarogya* (good health) and *Aanandha* (bliss) go hand in hand. SSS 14, 287-88

If there is a boil on the body, we put some ointment on it and cover it with a bandage until the whole thing heals. If you do not apply the ointment and tie the bandage around this boil, it is likely to become septic and cause great harm later on. Now and then we will have to clean it with pure water, apply the ointment again and put on a new bandage. In the same way, in our life, there is this particular boil which has come up in our body in the form of "I," "I," "I." If you want to really cure this boil of "I," you will have to wash it every day with the waters of love, apply the ointment of faith on it and tie the bandage of humility around it. The bandage of humility, the ointment of faith, and the waters of love will be able to cure this disease that has erupted with this boil of "I." SSS 18, 29

A sense of elation and exultation keeps the body free from ill-health. Evil habits in which men indulge are the chief cause of disease, physical as well as mental. Greed affects the mind; disappointment makes man depressed. SSS 14, 288

Health does not depend on medicine. Good words, good manners, good sight, good thoughts—these are essential. What can even powerful or costly medicines do if one is ill with bad thoughts and bad feelings. On the other hand, virtuous living, beneficial thoughts, elevating ideals and righteous conduct can confer not only health, but what is even more precious . . . the Ecstatic Awareness of Reality itself. SSS 15, 314

The one effective way to conquer all sources of physical and mental disease and debility is awareness of one's *Atmic* Reality. That will bring about an upsurge of Love and Light, for, when one recognizes that he is the *Atma*, he cognizes the same *Atma* in all, he shares the joy and grief of all, he partakes of the strength and weaknesses of all. SSS 15, 313

Grace

Shankaraachaarya stood before a house with his begging bowl. The old lady who lived there was struck by the effulgence on his face that betokened a realized soul; but she had nothing which she could drop in that bowl. She wrung her hands in despair; she cursed herself; she wondered why the distinguished mendicant had come to her door, instead of going to the doors of the affluent. Then she remembered she had a single myrobalan fruit [cherry plum], the last of a handful she had plucked from a tree in the jungle a few days earlier. When she felt thirsty, she used to eat a fruit. She brought it out, and with tears flowing in her wrinkled cheeks, she dropped it into the bowl. Shankaraachaarya was touched by her contribution; the Lord willed; a shower of golden myrobalans fell in the yard in front of her hut. She was placed above want even without her asking for it. That is the way Grace works. SSS 7, 173-74

Gratitude

The Divine is recognised by gifted people in the vast, the magnificent, the beautiful, the mighty, the majestic, the awesome. But, for the generality of mankind, the consciousness that each one is a miracle sustained by God, that each breath is a witness of God's Providence, that each event is proof of His Presence, comes but rarely in life. SSS 15, 190

The first step in Dharma is gratitude; the first duty of the child is reverence to the parents. When the first step is absent, ascent is impossible. SSS 6, 52

You may be able to pay back any debt; but, the debt you owe to your mother, you never can repay. SSS 9, 132

Humility

In the ward in which Einstein was living, there was a girl who was weak in mathematics and was repeatedly failing in that subject. A friend suggested to her that if she went to Einstein, the greatest living mathematician, he would help her to learn the subject well. The girl approached Einstein, and he readily agreed to give her tuition everyday. The girl was immensely grateful and gained confidence from Einstein's offer. The girl's mother, who had observed her daughter going to the great mathematician for tuition everyday, felt that the little girl was wasting Einstein's time by asking him to teach her elementary mathematics. She went one day to Einstein and apologised to him for her daughter's intrusion on his valuable time. Einstein told her: "Do not think I am just teaching mathematics to her. I am learning as many things from her as I am teaching her." Einstein was conscious that people who might excel in some subject might be lacking in general knowledge or common sense and knowledge of worldly matters. Even though he was a great scientist, he did not disdain to learn quite a few things from a young schoolgirl. This readiness to learn from any person or source is the real mark of greatness. SSS 20, 150-51

Just as sparrows during a storm fly towards a warm shelter, man too must take shelter in the Divine Principle to escape from the storms of life. He will be welcomed by the Divine, only when, as Jesus said, he becomes a child. Allow the children to come to me, he said. Children have no strong wishes to run after; they have no overpowering passion of hate or greed; so they are embodiments of Peace. SSS 7, 125

Joy

Once Buddha set out to seek alms. He was approaching a village where there were a number of devotees of Buddha. At that time some wicked persons confronted him on the way and abused Buddha in various ways. Buddha sat on a rock nearby without proceeding with his journey. He addressed his traducers: "Dear children, what is the pleasure you derive from abusing me?" Without giving the reasons, they continued abusing him in worse terms. Buddha sat down saying, "If abusing me gives you pleasure, enjoy at yourselves." Exhausted by their abuse, they were preparing to leave. At that time, Buddha told them, "I stayed here all the time because if I had gone to the village, my devotees there would not have spared you, if you had indulged in all this abuse before them. It is to save you from this calamity that I had put up with all your abuse, given you a free rein and stayed here." "If we want to please others, we have to do many things and even spend a lot of money. I am happy that today without incurring any expense or taking any trouble I could give so much pleasure to all of you! What a fine day for me!" exclaimed Buddha. "You have derived joy from abusing me. So, I am the cause of your joy. I have given you satisfaction thereby. To bring comfort and happiness to people, many build choultries, dig wells, or do other charitable acts. But without undertaking any of these acts, I have been able to give great satisfaction to these evil-minded men. This is a great achievement, indeed," observed Buddha. SSS 17, 130-31

How can things or events that do not last confer joy that lasts? SSS 15, 125

As a matter of fact, there is more joy in the actual doing than in the result that accrues. This must be your experience. All the elaborate arrangements that the master of the house makes for a wedding in the family: the reception, the feeding, the illumination, the music, these are thrilling while they are being planned and executed; but they do not give so much pleasure, once the thing is done. In the end, when the bills come, they might even cause disgust and grief! So it must be easy to discard the fruits of action, provided you spend some thought upon the process of Karma, and the worth of the fruit.
SSS 1, 127

All the joy you crave for is in you. But, like a man who has vast riches in the iron chest, but, who has no idea where the key is, you suffer. Hear properly the instructions, dwell upon them in the silence of meditation, practise what has been made clear therein; then, you can secure the key, open the chest and be rich in joy. SSS 9, 15

In fact, all that a man does, is, ultimately traceable to this urge—the urge to earn self-satisfaction. A man builds a house, writes a book, enters a job, executes a plan—all because he gets joy therefrom. The cuckoo coos sweetly, and derives joy therefrom, far more than those who happen to listen. The rose blooms on the plant, because of an inner urge, not an outer prompting. The father fondles his baby and receives thereby more joy than he ever gives. The various disciplines undergone by *saadhakas* (spiritual aspirants), monks, ascetics, and those on the march along the path of self-knowledge are all adopted and adhered to, because they give joy to oneself, and fulfill an inner need. SSS 12, 244

Liberation

A king was once out hunting in the forest and while pursuing a fleeing stag, he fell into a forsaken well which was very deep. No one of his retinue knew of his plight, for the stag had taken him far away into the woods, before his men could get trace of him. Luckily, even as he fell, he grasped the root of a tree that was hanging aloof from the side of the well, and thus escaped the death that yawned underneath. After a few agonizing hours, he heard some one reciting aloud the names of the Lord, near the mouth of the well. It was a holy man, and when he caught the faint echo of the unfortunate king's cry, he let down a rope and called out to the King to hold on to it tight, so that he might be pulled up into safety. The question now before the King was—Root or Rope?

Of course, the root helped him to survive, but, it had value only until the rope was offered. It would be folly to stick to the root even after the rope was ready to save. The root must be appreciated, but, thankfulness should not be exaggerated into attachment. *Samsaara* or worldly existence is like the root; the rope is the secret of liberation, through some *Mahaavaakyaa* (sacred utterance of Truth), that discloses in a flash the Truth.
SSS 5, 61

The secret of liberation lies, not in the mystic formula that is whispered in the ear and rotated on the rosary; it lies in the stepping out into action, the walking forward in practice, the pious pilgrim route and the triumphant reaching of the Goal. The best Guru is the Divine in you; yearn for hearing His Voice, His *Upadhesh* [counsel]. If you seek worldly Gurus, you will have to run from one to another, like a rat caught inside a drum, which flees to the right when the drummer beats on the left and to the left when he beats the right! Be aware of God and His overpowering Love, whatever you do or say. SSS 7b, 26

Embodiments of the Divine! Do not take it amiss, for, I am telling this only out of the fullness of my love. There are many nowadays who go about with various short-cuts to liberation, paths which they have marked out and are determined to preach, attracting disciples and forming groups; they concoct these out of *Hatha yoga, Kriyaa yoga, Raaja yoga*, and some thin *Vedhaantha* and then, start out as guides and leaders. But, the fruits they confer are only flippant and flimsy; they are not lasting or truly liberating. *Bhakthi yoga* alone, as laid down and practised through the centuries, can save and sustain. God can be realised only through love. Without love in the heart, God will not reside in the desert. Other paths develop conceit, separate man from man, man from beast. They contract, they do not reach out, they shrink your sphere of awareness of the Divine! Love is expansion, and expansion is Divine Life. Sow Love; it blossoms as compassion and tolerance; it yields the fruit of Peace *(Shaanthi).* SSS 7b, 142-43

Love

This day is the Festival of Light; that is to say, of Love. Knowledge too is praised as light, but it is often a clouding fog, a weapon of offence, a burden on the head, a drag on the hand of charity, a shackle on the feet. It ripens into a liberator only when it is earned through love and put into practice through love. Love alone gives Light. SSS 7b, 75

Once it happened that Krishna, Balaraama and Saathyaki who were quite little boys at that time, scarcely four or five years old, strayed into a thick jungle, all alone, when darkness fell, and there was no way of reaching Gokulam! Of course, as you must have guessed already, it was a stratagem of Krishna; even at that age, he would do nothing without a deep purpose behind it, and the purpose would invariably be teaching some one some good lesson. They decided to spend the night just where they were; Krishna put fright into them, with his descriptions of ghosts, ghouls and demons roaming in search of human prey. He proposed that two shall sleep for three hours at a stretch while the other one kept watch.

It was Saathyaki's duty to keep awake and be on the lookout, from 7 to 10; Balaraama was to be vigilant from 10 to 1 a.m. Krishna was to start his part of the duty at 1 and keep on till 4. Saathyaki sat up to 10 and Balaraama and Krishna laid themselves on beds of dried leaves and slept soundly. Meanwhile a demon did actually present himself, before the little Saathyaki. He fell upon the boy who resisted heroically dealing and receiving hammer-strokes with fists, with a good number of clawing and biting in between. The demon had to retreat at last, leaving Saathyaki badly mauled, but, happy. The two brothers were sound asleep; they had not been disturbed in the least by the noise of the encounter. Saathyaki had met blow with blow, and dealt injury for injury. At 10 he awakened Balaraama and stretched his body on the heap of leaves, as if nothing had happened. The demon invited Balaraama too for combat and had to retreat humiliated, because Balaraama too was as fierce as he, and his blows were even more terrible than

Saathyaki's. Balaraama too curled himself into the bed at 1 a.m., after waking up Krishna who was to keep watch until . . . 4 a.m.

The demon came roaring like a wounded tiger, and advanced ferociously at the little Divine Boy. Krishna turned his sweet charming face at him, and rewarded him with a lovely smile. That smile disarmed the demon; the longer he came under its influence, the weaker became his vengeance and venom. At last, the demon became as docile as a lamb; when the other two woke, they were surprised at the victory that Krishna had won by the weaponry of Love. You cannot destroy anger by anger, cruelty by cruelty, hatred by hatred. Anger can be subdued only by forbearance; cruelty can be overcome only by non-violence; hatred yields only to charity and compassion. SSS 11, 299-300

The Grace of God cannot be won through the gymnastics of reason, the contortions of Yoga or the denials of asceticism. Love alone can win it, Love that needs no requital, Love that knows no bargaining, Love that is paid gladly, as tribute to the All-loving, Love that is unwavering. Love alone can overcome obstacles, however many or mighty. There is no strength more effective than purity, no bliss more satisfying than love, no joy more restoring than *bhakthi* (devotion), no triumph more praiseworthy than surrender. SSS 11, 75

Expansion is Love. Expansion is the essence of Love. Love is God. Live in Love. That is the Dheepaavali Message I give you. When a lamp is lit from another, there are two where there was but one. The first one did not stop emitting light. You can light a million lamps from one; but, yet, the first will not suffer a jot! Love too is like this. Share it with a million, it will still be as bright as when it was alone. There is another lesson too which the illuminations on Dheepaavali Day tend to teach. Each house in the street lights a few lamps and keeps them on the door sill, the parapet wall, the gate, the porch, the well, and, what is the effect? The town is filled with light, the residents are happy, the children dance in glee, and the sky shines in the glow of earthly joy. Light spreads; it mingles with the light from other sources of light, it has no boundaries, no prejudices, no favourites. You may not like your neighbour. But the light from the lamp on your verandah shines hand in hand with the light from the lamp on his verandah! You cannot keep it back! SSS 7b, 76

As a lump of sugar sweetens every drop of water in the cup, the eye of love makes every person in the world friendly and attractive. SSS 7, 133

Your innate quality of love has enabled you to share in joy and peace. Love makes you all theists. You have to be labeled an atheist, if you have no love in you, however demonstrative your religiosity may be! If you believe that you can win the Grace of God by means of vows, fasts, feasts and recitation of hymns of praise, offering of flowers, etc., you are woefully mistaken. Love alone is the *sine qua non.* SSS 11, 81

Love must be regulated and directed by intelligence and discrimination. Or else, it may cause even injury and defeat.

When a person saw a fish struggling on a river bank because the waters receded leaving it high and dry, he sympathised with its plight and brought it home wrapped in his handkerchief. He found it struggling even when he put it to bed; so, he gave it a few teaspoonfuls of hot coffee. The poor fish could not survive such ignorant kindness! It died. If only he had put it back into the river, it could have lived happily; even if you put it in the bowl studded with gems, it would be miserable. SSS 11, 262

Without Love the Universe is naught. The highest Love makes us aware of the Lord in every one. The Lord is equally present in all. Life is Love; Love is Life. Without God, deprived of God, nothing and nobody can exist. We live on and through the Divine Will. It is His will that operates as Love in each of us. It is He who prompts the prayer, "Let all the worlds be happy." For, He makes us aware that the God we adore, the God we love, the God we live by, is in every other being as Love. Thus Love expands and encompasses all creation. Looking a little closer, we discover that life itself is Love. They are not two but one. Love is the very nature of life, as burning is the nature of fire, or wetness of water, or sweetness of sugar. SSS 15, 206-07

In the process of realising this state of Supreme Love, several opponents have to be overcome. Foremost among these are the six "enemies"--*Kama* (passion), *Krodha* (hatred), *Lobha* (greed), *Moha* (delusion), *Mada* (pride), *Maatsaryam* (envy). If one manages to overcome these six enemies, he is confronted with eight forms of pride, which stand in the way of his spiritual progress. Among these are pride of wealth, of physical strength, youth, beauty, scholarship, power or penance. These different forms of pride lead man away from his real goal. Modern man is filled with one or other of these forms of pride. SSS 19, 78

If there is no love in the heart, there is no use in doing anything whatsoever. SSS 18, 8

Oneness

Do not walk in front of Me. I may not follow you. Don't walk behind Me. I may not lead you. Walk beside Me and be My friend. If you attempt to walk in front of Me, you may be taking the wrong path. If you walk behind Me, you may possibly desert Me. Walk abreast of Me. Then there is no chance of your going astray or away from Me, because I am with you. The inner meaning of this is: "You and I are one." Divinity is omnipresent. The Divinity is the Indweller in every being. That being the case, there is no need for you to go in front or walk behind. Take the Divine with you, wherever you go. This is the true mark of the *Sadhaka.* SSS 19, 191-92

When the four bulls that grazed in the jungle were united and watchful of each other's safety (for they felt they were all One) the tiger dared not approach them; but, when discord broke them and created out of the One, four separate individuals, they were attacked one by one, and destroyed by the tiger. That is the fate of those who feel separate. SSS 6, 32

When the wind agitates the serene waters of a lake, wavelets dance all over its face, and a thousand suns sparkle. When calm descends and the waters are still, the [reflection] of the Sun within the lake is one full image.

When one fixes one's entire attention on the Sun instead of on the images and the water that caused them, there is only the one Sun that is Real. The sparkling little images in the agitated lake represent the symbol of *Dhwaitha* (duality); the complete image in the depths of the serene lake is the symbol of *Visishtaadwaitha* (qualified dualism); the One Sun which is reflected as one or many is the *Adhwaithic* (non-dualistic) Truth. This fact is clearly revealed in the three statements made one after the other by Jesus: "I am the Messenger of God," "I am the Son of God," and "I and my Father are One." The three statements are revelations of the *Dhwaithic, Visishtaadhwaithic* and *Adwaithic* points of view.
SSS 13, 106

Differences that strike you while you cast your eyes are illusory; you have not yet developed the vision that makes you apprehend the unity which is the truth of all the seeming diversity, that is all! The fault is in you, not the world. The world is One; but, each takes it to mean what pleases him most! The world is One, but, each sees it from his own angle and so, it appears as if it has multiple faces. SSS 9, 28

Do not distinguish between one fellow-pilgrim and another on the basis of caste, creed or colour, and do not divide them into friends or foes. Recognize only the common traits, the uniting efforts, the basic Divinity. Rich and poor, scholar and illiterate—these are distinctions that do not hold for long, for they are but outer frills. A flower radiates fragrance and charm whether held in the right hand or the left. It does not limit that gift to some and deny it to others. Everyone who comes near, is blessed. SSS 13, 106

Today there is a great need for every one to dwell upon the axioms that Dharmaraja, the eldest of the Pandava brothers, kept before himself. When Krishna asked him one day where his brothers were, he replied, “Some of them are in Hasthinaapura city and the others in the forest.” Krishna was visibly surprised, He said, “Dharmaraja! What has happened to your brains? All of you, the five brothers, are here in the forest as you know. None is in the city of Hasthinaapura!” Dharmaraja replied, “Pardon me, Lord! We are 105 brothers in all.” Krishna pretended that the statement was wrong. He recounted the names of the five and queried the reason why he added a hundred more. “My father’s sons are five; his brother, the blind Dhritharaashtra has a hundred sons. When we fight with them, we are five and they hundred. But when we don’t, we are a hundred and five.”
SSS 14, 236-37

Those who argue that the Spiritual path is for the individual one, and that society should not be involved in it, are committing a great mistake. It is like insisting that there is light inside the house, and saying that it does not matter if there is darkness outside. SSS 19, 233

It should also be realised that nothing in creation is intended for the exclusive use of any one person. We should therefore discard the feeling: "These things have been given for my exclusive use, they are my own." SSS 18, 178

Parental Modeling

When the father asks the child to tell someone at the door that he is not at home, or when he asks its brother to reply to a phone call, that he has gone out, the vice of dishonesty is implanted in the child. Do not burden the tender brains with all kinds of lumber, information that can never be put to use, facts that warp and twist truth, etc. Teach them only as much as they can use beneficially and as much as can be of direct help to them in their lives. Train character more than brains. SSS 9, 9

The parents have to be imbued with faith in the basic truths of this Universal Religion. They must be seen worshipping at the family altar, meditating in silence, forgiving the lapses of others, sympathizing with pain and grief; they should not be seen by the children as worried, helpless, discontented and distressed, as if they had no God to lean upon, no inner reserves of strength and courage to fall back upon. SSS 7, 78

Peace

By peace, Western countries mean the interval between two wars, when vigorous efforts are made to avenge the insult of defeat, and consolidate the spoils of victory and prepare for the next round! That is no peace! SSS 9, 119

Renounce and win peace; have and win troubles. There was a man living in a ramshackle hut when a huge . . . storm came along threatening to scatter it to the far corners; he sat inside and prayed to Vayudeva (windgod). "Oh Vayu! Abate thy fury," but the storm raged wild and furious. He prayed to Hanuman, the son of the wind god Vayu. "O Hanuman, soften the fury of your father and save this poor fellow's shelter," and the storm blew with even more ferocity. Then he prayed to Rama to command His servant, Hanuman, to persuade the wind god to reduce His overpowering sweep. He found that too had no effect. So, he came out of the hut and coolly said, "Let it be pulled asunder and lifted by the storm out of sight. I do not care." Thus, he got his peace of mind back. SSS 4, 181

Practice

Jesus pleaded for Compassion. Compassion was His Message. He was sorely distressed at the sight of the poor. This day, Jesus is worshipped, but His teachings are neglected. Sai is being worshipped, but His teachings are neglected. Everywhere, pomp, pageantry, hollow exhibitionism! Lectures, Lectures, Lectures! No activity, no love, no *seva* [service]. Heroes while lecturing, zeros while putting what is said into practice. SSS 15, 210

Christmas Day, 1981

The *Jnana* [wisdom] has to be put into practice. Otherwise, it is useless. Once the deers of the forest gathered in a great assembly and discussed their own cowardice in the face of the pursuing hounds. They argued, "Why should we, who are equipped with fleeter feet and sharp antlers be afraid of these insignificant dogs?" At last, a resolution was moved and passed that no deer should henceforth flee before hounds but, even while the cheering was going on, they heard the distant baying of the hounds and, not one stayed there; all . . . fled as fast as their legs could carry them! The resolution could not be put into practice! SSS 3, 100-01

When the word "Lamp" is uttered, darkness does not vanish; when a patient is told of the properties of a drug, his illness is not cured by attentive listening; when a man suffering the agonies of penury is told of the various ways in which funds can help him to overcome it, he does not feel a bit relieved; a hungry man is hungry, even after hearing a tasty description of a magnificent banquet. If *Sanaathana Dharma* (the eternal religion) is extolled to the skies, as the cure for all the individual, social and national discontent prevalent among mankind, the discontent will not decrease a bit. You must extol it with faith; extol it out of the depth of your experience. You have to experience it and stand witness to its validity; you have to attain the state of perfect and lasting joy. Instead, you have ignored the cure and thus heightened the disease. SSS 7, 37

If you are told that Nachiketa did this or Svetaketu said that, of what avail is it? Unless you adopt them as your ideals, exemplars, guides, these *Upanishadhs* and scriptural texts are only fairy tales! Try to understand their steadfastness, their faith, their sense of values, their virtues and their uprightness. And yearn to acquire them. Then only can we have another Nachiketa and another Svetaketu. Or else, in the entire course of human history, there will be only one Nachiketa and one Svetaketu! SSS 7, 109-110

Most of you hear me say these things over and over again, year after year. But few take even the first step in *saadhana*. You ask that I should go on speaking, and you take down notes of what I say for the purpose of reading them again. But, without practice, all this is sheer waste. SSS 5, 191

True human greatness consists of a continuous series of tiny acts executed with absolute sincerity and largeness of heart.
SSS 12, 256

Purity

Life has to be an incessant process of repair and reconstruction, of discarding evil and developing goodness. Paddy grains have to discard the husk in order to become consumable rice. Cotton has to be reformed as yarn to become wearable cloth. Even gold nuggets have to undergo the crucible and get rid of alloys. Man too must purify his instincts, impulses, passions, emotions and desires so that he can progress in good thoughts, deeds and words. SSS 19, 206

Your *saadhana* must avoid becoming like drawing water from a well in a cane basket! You get no water however often you may dip and pull the basket up. Each vice is a hole in the bucket. Keep the heart pure, keep it whole. SSS 9, 5

Renunciation

Renounce the idea of your being separate; see in all beings, yourself; and yourself in all beings. That is the highest renunciation, the renunciation of the sense of ego, which makes you cling to this temporary habitation, this bundle of bone and flesh, this shell with a Name and Form. Spiritual exercise consists of two things: Contemplation of God, and discovery of one's innate nature or reality. SSS 7b, 47

Self-Confidence

Without self-confidence no achievement is possible. SSS 7, 187

The ultimate step of self-realization depends upon the base of self-confidence. You must therefore develop, as a first step, confidence in your own self. Without having and developing confidence in your own self, if all the time you are talking of some power being with someone and some other power being with someone else, if in this way you travel all the time and depend upon power which is with someone else, when are YOU going to acquire any power and confidence in your OWN self? Peace and bliss are within you; they are not something which is external to you. You may think of going to the Himalayas for getting peace; but your mind may be left behind in the city. How are you going to get peace? You have brought your body to India; but still, if you have the same habits which you are used to in America, what is the use of bringing the body to India? Body is not the essential thing. The transformation should come in your mind, the change should come in your mind. SSS 13, 30

Service

Krishna was known to all as almighty, all-knowing, all-encompassing and all-fulfilling. Yet, the enthusiasm to do *seva* [service] prompted him to approach Dharmaraja, the eldest of the Pandava brothers, on the eve of the magnificent *Raajsooya Yaaga* he had planned to celebrate and offered to take up *seva* of any kind. He suggested that he might be given the task of cleaning the dining hall after the guests had partaken of the feast! Krishna insisted on outer cleanliness and inner cleansing. Clean clothes and clean minds are the ideal combination.

During the battle of Kurukshetra, which climaxed the Mahaabhaaratha story, Krishna served as the "driver" of the chariot of Arjuna throughout the day on the field, and when dusk caused the adjournment of the fight, he led the horses to the river, gave them a refreshing bath and applied healing balms to the wounds suffered by them during the fierce fray. He mended the reins and the harness and rendered the chariot battleworthy for another day. SSS 15, 167

The person who serves is the person served; you serve yourself when you serve another. You serve another because his suffering causes you anguish, and by relieving it, you want to save yourselves from that anguish. Unless you have that anguish, your service will be hollow and insincere. SSS 7, 205

The pain that another suffers from, which you seek to assuage, is really your own pain; when you stop his pain, it is your pain that stops. SSS 16, 36

Whenever you are serving another and relieving his distress, remember it is your own distress that you are relieving. A cow was caught in a bog and it was floundering helplessly. A throng of idlers was watching its struggles with great relish. A *Sanyaasin* (monk) passing along the road saw the unfortunate animal; he removed his shirt. He threw away his head cover; he jumped into the slush and lifted the cow on to the bank, in spite of its kicks and frantic movements. The throng laughed at his bravado and weightlifting prowess, and someone asked him, "Why could you not go your way, unconcerned?"

The *Sanyassin* replied, "The picture of that cow's agony cut into my heart; I could not go one step further. I had to get rid of the pain in my heart. This was the cure for that pain. I did it to save myself, not so much to save the cow." You serve yourself; you harm yourself, when you gloat on the harm you have inflicted on another. There is no ANOTHER! Only those who have reached that stage of spiritual progress have a right to advise on service. SSS 7, 129-30

When the child in the cradle starts weeping and wailing the mother who is on the terrace of the house will run down the steps to fondle it and feed it. She will not stop to discover whether the wail was in the correct key or on the proper note! So also, the Supreme Mother of the Universe will come down from Her Sovereign Throne to fondle, caress and console Her child, provided the yearning comes spontaneously from a full heart, a pure heart. She will not investigate the correctness or otherwise of the pronunciation of the *manthra* or the perfection of the picture formed in the mind of the Divine Ideal yearned for. It is the feeling in the heart that is the crucial test—not the length of time devoted or the amount of money spent. SSS 7b, 106-07

Do not judge others to decide whether they deserve your service. Find out only whether they are distressed; that is enough credential. SSS 7a, 209

Ostentation in rendering service is totally out of place. It will only inflate the ego. You should render service to the limit of your capacity, neither more nor less. SSS 17, 77

What you offer should be within your capability. The person to whom it is offered should be deserving and should be capable of making proper use of what is offered. To make offerings beyond one's capacity to undeserving persons or to persons incapable of putting them to proper use is like offering a golden toy to a child or presenting a knife to a lunatic. It may have many undesirable consequences. SSS 16, 137

Zeal and zest are more efficient instruments for service than gifts and donations. They give one man the energy of ten.
SSS 9, 97

Those of you who have had the privilege of serving your unfortunate brothers and sisters will stand witness to what I am saying now; there is no discipline equal to Service to smother the ego and to fill the heart with genuine joy. To condemn service as demeaning and inferior is to forgo these benefits. A wave of service, if it sweeps over the land, catching everyone in its enthusiasm, will be able to wipe off the mounds of hatred, malice and greed that infest the world. SSS 9, 95

Silence

One of the first principles of straight living is: Practise silence. For the Voice of God can be heard in the region of your heart only when the tongue is stilled and the storm is stilled, and the waves are calm. There will be no temptation for others to shout when you talk to them in whispers. Set the level of the tone yourself: as low as possible, as high as necessary to reach to outermost boundary of the circle you are addressing. Conserve sound, since it is the treasure of the element *Aakaasha* (space), an emanation from God Himself. Reason can prevail only when arguments are advanced without the whipping up of sound. Silence is the speech of the spiritual seeker. Soft sweet speech is the expression of genuine Love. Hate screeches; fear squeals; conceit trumpets. But, love sings lullabies, it soothes, it applies balm. Practise the vocabulary of Love; unlearn the language of hate and contempt. SSS 7a, 207-08

Sincerity

If you have no *shraddha* (earnestness) you cannot achieve anything, whatever other qualifications you may have. SSS 17, 13

Taking a Stand

Here is an example from the *Mahabharata*: Considering that war should be a great universal calamity, Dharmaraja (the eldest of the Pandavas) appealed to Krishna to go as an ambassador of peace to the Kauravas. Entering the audience hall of Duryodhana, Krishna described at length the disastrous consequences of war. The great Acharyas—Bhishma, Drona, Kripa and Aswathama—who were present in the court, were intently listening to Krishna's words. But Krishna's appeal was of no use to them. Because of their long association with the wicked Kauravas, they became abettors in the crimes of Duryodhana and others.

Vidura, who was a witness to the evil that was being committed, resolved to oppose it. He pleaded with the Kauravas in many ways to listen to the wise words of Krishna. His appeal fell on deaf ears. Rather than stay amongst such evil-minded persons, Vidura felt that it was better to go on a pilgrimage, and left the country immediately. SSS 19, 186

When Silence is a Crime

Bhishma, Drona and others, having been beneficiaries of the sustenance provided by the wicked Kauravas, chose to be loyal to them and stayed on. All of them were great preceptors. They knew well the distinction between righteousness and evil. They had enquired into the nature of the eternal and the permanent. Of what avail was all that knowledge? When it came to practising what they knew, all their knowledge was of no use. In the final outcome, all of them met with the same end in the great war as the evil-minded Kauravas.

Krishna looked upon those who, even if they were good in themselves, did not oppose unrighteousness and injustice committed in their presence when they had the capacity to do so, as actual participants in the crimes. When evil and injustice and violence are being perpetrated, if individuals look on unconcerned, they must be regarded as accomplices in the crimes. In the end they also suffer as much as the criminals. By their passive association, they provide encouragement to the evildoers.

Failure to Resist Evil is an Offence

When the good are associated with the wicked and do not oppose them, they share the responsibility for the deeds of the evil-doers. The Divine destroys even those who either do not oppose or remain passive while injustice and wrong-doing are perpetrated. The Divine will not consider whether they are learned or ignorant, wise or unwise. If they are learned or wise, why did they not stand up for truth and justice? Why did they remain silent? It means they are tainted by the same guilt. The failure to resist evil is their offence. It is only when we resist acts of unrighteousness and injustice and try to put down malpractices in society that we can claim to be assisting in the task of restoring Dharma. SSS 19, 186-87

In *Treta Yuga,* Ravana's brother, Vibhishana, could not put up with the wrong deeds being done by Ravana. Opposing these actions, he tried to correct Ravana in all possible ways. But when his efforts failed and he had no alternative, he sought refuge at the feet of the embodiment of Dharma, Sri Rama. The prime offender was Ravana alone. But in the war with Rama, all . . . who supported him or sided with him, perished with him. They paid the penalty for their abetment of his crime.

Whoever may commit an offence, whether a son, a relation or a close associate, one will be free from the taint of being accessory to the crime only if he opposes the wrong action and tries to correct the offender. If on the contrary, he allows it or encourages it to be done, he will be guilty of abetment. SSS 19, 187-88

During the Kurukshethra battle, [Dharmaraja] was persuaded to utter a white lie, a subterfuge which he thought was excusable, though it was not [one hundred] percent honest. In order to kill Drona, the master archer and General on the opposite side, they had to somehow trick him into discarding his bow; so they planned a subterfuge. They named a war elephant after Drona's son, Aswatthama. Then, they killed it. Immediately, within the hearing of Drona, the Pandava army was asked to shout in glee, "Aswatthama is killed—the elephant," which was strictly true. But, while the soldiers were repeating the words, "the elephant," drums were beaten, bugles were sounded, trumpets pealed, so that Drona heard only the first three words. Naturally, he took them to mean that his son had met with his death from enemy hands. Drona was heavily laden with grief; his hands could not wield the bow and the arrow, as deftly as usual; at that moment, he was overwhelmed and slain. For this one sin that he had encouraged, the only one in his life, Dharamaraja had to spend a few minutes in Hell, say the Puranas. Such is the consequence of departing from Sathya [Truth] even by a hair's breadth.

Listen to the sequel. When the emissaries of the other world were escorting Dharmaraja after death to Hell, for this nominal sojourn, the denizens of Hell suddenly felt a coolness and a fragrance in the air they breathed, a strange peace and joy, a thrill and exhilaration which they had never hoped to enjoy. That was the consequence of the holy soul approaching the region of terror and torture. The unfortunate sinners gathered around Dharmaraja to be soothed and comforted by his very sight. When Dharmaraja was directed to turn back towards Heaven (the term of his sentence was soon over) the populace of Hell cried out to him to prolong his stay. They were reluctant to go back to the heat and the pain. Hearing their piteous wail, Dharmaraja declared that he was surrendering to them all the merit that had earned Heaven for him; he was willing to stay with them! But that great act of renunciation not only benefited the suffering creatures, it gave Dharmaraja a greater lease of life in Heaven [later], and a more honoured place there. Life is best spent in alleviating pain, assuaging distress, and promoting peace and joy.

The service of man is more valuable than what you call "service to God." God has no need of your service. Please man; you please God . . . When you serve man, you serve God. SSS 6, 18-19

There are some other things you can do to lead you to the consummation. For example, adhere strictly to truth. . . . The mind is cleansed by Truth. Truth is the great purifier. It admits no dirt or sin, no defect or deceit. Falsehood pollutes the tongue of the speaker, the ear of the listener and the air which carries it from tongue to tympanum. There are beneficent and maleficent sounds, and they produce corresponding echoes in the atmosphere. Words that emanate from faith in God and the humility it fosters will render the atmosphere pure, while those trumpeted by vanity and execrated by nihilism and atheism will contaminate it. SSS 9, 144

Truth is a word that is frequently used on platforms, but the concept is still very hazy and often mistakenly interpreted. In reality, man is afraid of probing into his own truth, lest his pet opinions and attitudes be proved hollow and dangerous. As a result, his actions and thoughts pursue disturbing and discordant paths.

What exactly is truth? Is it the description of a "thing seen" as one has seen it, without exaggeration or under-statement? No. Or, the narration of an incident in the same words as one has heard it narrated? No. Truth elevates; it holds forth ideals; it inspires the individual and society. It is the Light that illumines Man's path to God. SSS 14, 250

Vision

The world appears dual according to our likes and dislikes. If we like a thing, it is good for us. If we dislike it, it is bad.
SSS 15, 212

Wisdom

There is a tale told of old that Wisdom and Wealth once quarreled loud and long about their relative importance. Wealth argued that without it, the body will be weak, the brain hazy and wisdom a will-o-the-wisp. Wisdom retorted that without it man cannot even distinguish wealth from non-wealth or know how to earn it or use it. The Soul intervened and told them that they were both equally important, but only when properly used. Wealth without wisdom becomes an instrument of exploitation and tyranny; wisdom without wealth becomes mere fantasy and a bundle of blueprint. Use makes them worthwhile; misuse makes them disastrous.

It is like the knife in the hands of a maniac, which becomes an instrument for murder; in the hands of a surgeon, it becomes an instrument which saves a life. Are you doing good with wealth? Are you benefiting others by means of wisdom?—that is the test. SSS 11, 344-45

Surrender

One day, Krishna developed a type of agonising stomach-ache! The sage, Naaradha, happened to put in his appearance and witness the suffering. He was upset, and he prayed that he may be commissioned to bring to Him the drug that will cure the pain. "There is just one drug that can assuage it, but can you bring it for me?" asked Krishna. Naaradha said, "Tell me, it will be done!" "Bring for me the dust of the feet of any real devotee; that will stop the pain," replied the Lord.

Naaradha moved out very fast to procure it, but at the door, he remembered that he himself was the most earnest and sincere devotee. So, he turned back and suggested to the Lord that the dust of his own feet may be used. But, the Lord said, "No; no. Egoism has tainted it, and so it has contaminated the drug." So, Naaradha had perforce to go abroad and seek it from others who he knew as great devotees. But, no one of them gave him the dust! Some were afraid, some were ashamed, some withdrew fearing sacrilege, some asserted they were not devotees, being only mere aspirants of Grace.

Then, Naaradha went into Brindhaavan where the simple *Gopees* were. He told them of his plight and Krishna's pain. At this, each one of them collected the dust of their feet and within seconds, Naaradha's hands were full of packets. "Rush with these; may the pain cease!"—that was their response. The petty little ideas of superiority or inferiority, of pride or humility, of shame or fear, did not enter their minds. "The Lord is in pain; it must be cured," that was all they knew and cared to know. They did not stop to inquire whether the Lord could really be suffering, whether the dust of their feet had any curative property, whether the mission on which Naaradha had come had any deeper meaning for them or the world! They heard, they gave, they prayed, they were happy. They felt the pain that Krishna had; they responded to the command. They were all equally affected, and their reactions were all equally prompt and sincere.

You must surrender your judgement to the Lord; then, the Lord will assume full responsibility and be the guardian, guide and motive power. SSS 7b, 131-32

When the yearning for Liberation has become intense beyond expression, man can set aside all social conventions, worldly norms and codes of conduct, that do not subserve that high purpose. SSS 6, 39

Regulation, strict regulation, is essential up to a certain stage of individual development.

The aeroplane runs on wheels for some length on the ground, before it takes off into the air. You may say, "Why wheels for air-plane?" So too, when you reach a certain height in spiritual *saadhana*, rules and regulations can be folded up, as the pilot folds up the wheels when up in the air. SSS 11, 139

There are three steps or stages in this journey. "I am YOURS"; "YOU are Mine!" and, finally, "I am YOU!" Every saadhaka has to walk from one to the other, and reach the journey's end. Move on, don't halt. It is good to be born in a church, but it is not good to die in it. Grow and rescue yourselves from the limits and regulations, the doctrines that fence your freedom of thought, the ceremonials and rites that restrict and re-direct. Reach the point where churches do not matter, where all roads end, from where all roads run. SSS 9, 78

When you intend going on a journey, you hand over the keys of your car to the chauffer and sit in comfort and security in the back-seat, forgetting the possible troubles on the way. You have surrendered your life into the hands of that man, his intelligence, alertness and skill. Some men do not fully surrender; they are too egoistic for that! They interrupt him every minute with tips, hints, and suggestions about driving; with questions and doubts regarding the condition of the car or the road! And, so, they confuse him and confound his confidence so much that they inflict accidents upon themselves! Be steady, have Faith, and reach the goal safe. Life is the car, your heart is the key. God is the *saarathi* (chauffeur). Surrender to Him and be rid of further bother. Travel safe and arrive happy. SSS 11, 804

When the road ends, and the Goal is gained, the pilgrim finds that he has traveled only from himself to himself, that the way was long and lonesome, but the God that led him unto it was all the while in him, around him, with him, and beside him! He himself was always Divine. His yearning to merge in God was but the sea calling to the Ocean! Man loves, because He is Love! He craves for melody and harmony, because He is melody and harmony. He seeks Joy, for He is Joy. He thirsts for God, for he is composed of God, and he cannot exist without Him. SSS 8, 39

From the Full, the Full has emerged, leaving the Full ever Full. The Created is as full of the One as the One whose manifestation it is. The Experiencer is as Full as the Experienced. A grain of sand is as full as a star in the sky. The *Paramaathma,* who is the One Fullness, has willed mankind which is co-sharer of that Fullness. Man has to fulfil himself, half through the Grace of the effort and half through the Grace of the indwelling Divine. Awareness of this Fullness, escaping from the illusion of incompleteness, is the goal, the destination of human life. When man knows, visualises and experiences the Creator, he becomes as mighty, as majestic and as knowledgeable as the Creator. SSS 15, 27

Be lamps of love. That contains all. SSS 7b, 86

Glossary

Aukaasha—Space

Acharya, Aacharya—Spiritual teacher.

Adharma—Unrighteous conduct.

Agroygya—Good health.

Ananda, Aanandha—Bliss.

Arjuna—One of the Pandava brothers, a supreme archer, the one to whom Krishna revealed *The Bhagavad Gita*.

Atma—Self, Soul, Divine Spirit.

Avatar, Avathaar—Incarnation of God.

Bhakti—Devotion.

Bhagavad Gita, or *Geetha*—The Heart of Hindu teaching, Krishna instructing the Pandava, Arjuna.

Bhoga—enjoyment, the antithesis of Yoga.

Brahman—The Supreme Being, The Absolute Reality.

Chintha—anxiety.

Dharma—Righteousness, right action.

Dharmaraja—Eldest of the Pandava brothers and leader.

Dhyana, Dhyanna—Meditation.

Drona—Preceptor of the Pandava brothers, master archer, General on the Kaurava side during the Kurukshetra War.

Duryodhana—Eldest of the Kaurava brothers and leader most responsible for the Kurukshetra war.

Gopees, Gopikas—Simple cowherders, devotees of Krishna.

Guru—Spiritual guide.

Jnana, Jnaana—Knowledge of the Spirit, to obtain self-realization.

Kama—Passion.

Karma—Action, work, deed.

Krishna—A Hindu avatar, incarnation of God.

Krodha—Hatred.

Kurukshetra—The great war between good and evil, the Pandava brothers and their Kaurava cousins.

Lobha—Greed.

Maatsaryam—Envy.

Mada—Pride.

Mahabharata, Mahaabhaaratha—The Hindu epic written by Vyasa concerning the encounter between the Pandava brothers and their corrupted cousins, the Kauravas. *The Bhagavad Gita* or *Geetha*, is part of this epic.

Maya, Maaya—The illusory nature of the world.

Moha—Delusion.

Namasmarana, Naamasmarana—Repetition of one of the names of God.

Pandit, Pandith—A learned person.

Paramatma, Paramaathma—The Supreme Atma, the higher Self of God.

Pranava—Om, the most exalted syllable in the Vedas.

Prema—Love, Divine Love.

Puja, Puuja—worship.

Rama—A Hindu avatar, incarnation of God, chief character in *The Ramayana*.

Ramayana, Raamaayana—The Hindu epic written by Valmoki concerning the encounter between Rama and the evil Ravana.

Sadhaka, saadhaka—Spiritual aspirant.

Sadhana, Saadhana—Spiritual discipline, effort to attain God-realization.

Samsara, Samsaara—Worldly life.

Sanyasi, Sanyassin—Monk.

Sastras, Shaasthras—The Hindu scriptures revealing the teachings of the Rishis.

Sathya—Truth.

Satsang—Company of the good.

Seva—Service.

Shanti, Shaanti—Peace.

Shraddha—Earnestness.

Upadesh—Inner Divine counsel.

Vedas, Vedhas—The most ancient and holy Hindu scriptures.

Vedanta, Vedhaantha—The essence of the Vedas, embodied in the teachings of the Upanishads.

Yoga—Union with God, or the path to this union.

Sources

HUNDREDS OF BOOKS IN ENGLISH ALONE exist by or about Sathya Sai Baba. At last count, there were at least fourteen volumes of Baba's commentaries in *Summer Showers in Brindavan*, twenty-one volumes of his *Vahini* (Stream) series, and thirty-nine volumes of *Sathya Sai Speaks*. There are also numberless insights given by Baba to individual devotees.

Quotations in this book are from the first twenty volumes of *Sathya Sai Speaks*, Baba's discourses from 1953 to 1987, and are presented with the permission of the Chief Functionary of the Sri Sathya Sai Books & Publications Trust, Prasaanthi Nilayam, Anantapur District, Andhra Pradesh 515134, India.

Quotations are cited as follows: SSS, 5, 153, meaning *Sathya Sai Speaks*, volume 5, page 153.

Seekers are invited to read the entire volumes available through the webpages below.

International Sai Organization
Web: www.sathysai.org
Email: enquiry@sssbpt.org

Sathya Sai Baba Book Center of America
Web: www.sathyasaibooks.com

Sri Sathya Sai Book and Information Centre,
290 Merton Street, Toronto, ON
Canada M4S1A9
Web: www.saibooks.org
Email: saibooks@direct.ca

The first thirty volumes of Sathya Sai Speaks appear online at:

http://www.sathyasai.org/discour/sathyasaispeaks/sathyasaispeaks.html